Overthinking

How to Rewire your Mind and Control your Thoughts to Live a Stress-Free Life and Make Better Decisions Every Day

I0707077

Table of Contents

© **Copyright 2019 - All rights reserved.**

The contents of this book may not be reproduced, duplicated or transmitted without direct written permission from the author.

Under no circumstances will any legal responsibility or blame be held against the publisher for any reparation, damages, or monetary loss due to the information herein, either directly or indirectly.

Legal Notice:

This book is copyright protected. This is only for personal use. You cannot amend, distribute, sell, use, quote or paraphrase any part or the content within this book without the consent of the author.

Disclaimer Notice:

Please note the information contained within this document is for educational and entertainment purposes only. Every attempt has been made to provide accurate, up to date and reliable complete information. No warranties of any kind are expressed or implied. Readers acknowledge that the author is not engaging in the rendering of legal, financial, medical or professional advice. The content of this book has been derived from various sources. Please consult a licensed professional before attempting any techniques outlined in this book.

By reading this document, the reader agrees that under no circumstances is the author responsible for any losses, direct or indirect, which are incurred as a result of the use of information contained within this document, including, but not limited to, —errors, omissions, or inaccuracies.

Introduction

Have you ever wondered how some people sail through life, seemingly without a worry? Why are they so successful and happy? Why is life not that simple for you? Chances are you are guilty of overthinking and automatic negative thoughts. What are they and why do you have them?

This book will answer all your questions, and, more importantly, show you how to change the way you think. You can be that confident successful person who achieves their dream and who refuses to accept defeat. Read on and discover the world of positivity and success!

Chapter 1: Overthinking and How to stop It

Are you a worrier? Do you analyze every situation and then rethink it one more time? Worrying is not a medical condition but anxiety is. Overthinking is the steppingstone that joins the two.

Worrying and overthinking can cause you to miss out on so many things and can impede your social life. Are you missing out on new relationships because you over analyze every new person you meet? Does worry impact your work and cause you to underachieve? If worrying and overthinking is taking over your life try these tips to help you lessen your stress levels:

- Admit it: We as humans find it difficult to admit we have a problem, but this must be the first step to a solution. You need to acknowledge that worry and overthinking is part of your natural process and learn how to put the brakes on. Next time you find yourself overthinking a subject just take a pause and step away.

- Expand your horizons: We live in an amazing world and while nobody expects you to see it all we can all push our boundaries. Traveling is a great way to get new perspectives on life and gives you something to look forward to. Planning a trip is half the fun and the anticipation can be tangible. Give your brain a boost and plan a vacation, it doesn't have to be expensive or even lengthy. A night in a hotel can be a welcome distraction from troubles at home or even visiting a local tourist spot that you have never seen before. It's all about giving yourself a break from worrying and expanding your perspectives.

- Be Cynical: Your mind can be a terrible liar and fill your thoughts with untruths. Negative self-talk can fill you with fear and make you question every decision. The fact is just because your mind is telling you that worrying, and overthinking are positive actions and will lead to better decisions does not mean it is true. You need to take back the power of your own thoughts and replace them with positive ones.

- Take a picture: Do you often look back at old photos and remember the great times they represent? We now have that ability at our fingertips with our phones and other devices. Taking a quick snap of something beautiful or interesting helps us distract our thoughts and focus on a positive image. Photography is also a way to open your creative side and bring a balance to your day which is a perfect way to reduce stress.

- Put a time limit on it: Stopping worrying is a process that takes time. Try this simple exercise to limit the amount of time spent stressing. Give yourself a boundary, for instance, 5 mins to worry about work and do exactly that. Once the 5 minutes are up taking another 5 minutes to write down all your concerns and then rip up the paper and throw it away. Now is the time to move on, hopefully to something a lot more fun!

- Distract yourself: Worrying and overthinking is often caused by having too much time on your hands. If your mind starts to show signs of overthinking distract it with another activity. Keep a journal, do physical exercise or even calling someone to talk to. Whatever it takes to get yourself out of the moment and let the thoughts pass will work. Soon you will realize just how much time worrying and overthinking was wasting. Keeping busy will help you feel less anxious and lead a fulfilling life.

- Gardening: Studies have shown that people who get their hands dirty in the garden benefit from improved mental health, increased relaxation and mindfulness. Digging in soil and producing your own products gives you an outlet to vent your worries and excess thoughts. It also gives you a healthy sense of control, after all, if you don't put the effort into your plants will die. This is a pleasant balanced way to spend your time if you are prone to overthinking. You don't need a massive plot of land or even a garden to benefit from gardening. Try some seedlings in an old ice cube tray and then transfer to pots or a window pot. Use cooking water to act as a natural fertilizer and feel the satisfaction of growing your own plants!

- Exercise: Sometimes a physical workout can be the best cure for a worried mind. Concentrate instead of putting your body through a workout that will leave you energized yet tired. You can set your own exercise goals and do something great for your body at the same time. Exercise will also give your body the incentive to sleep better and fall asleep sooner. Overthinking often occurs at night so if your body is craving sleep after exercising you will not have the energy to worry!

- Be grateful: How often do we take the time to be grateful for what we have and give thanks for the life we live? We are constantly pushed to achieve more and move onwards and upwards and this can lead to worry and stress. Keep a journal of things you are grateful for and refer to it regularly. Whenever you start to feel unworthy or stuck in a rut you can gain satisfaction in reminding yourself what you have achieved in your life. Gratitude gives you a different perspective on life and when you think about what you are grateful for you will find there are fewer things to worry about.

- Relax: If music makes you relax then use it to distract you from worrying. Turn up the radio or put your favorite album on and lose yourself in the music. Maybe combine meditation with your music and sit for a while controlling your breathing and clearing your mind. Picture pleasant images and let your thoughts flow freely while breathing steadily and you will soon feel the calming effect it will have on you. Meditation can be an important part of your daily routine and can be practiced anywhere at any time.

- Help others: There is nothing more satisfying than helping other people and solving their problems. There are help-seekers all around you. The friend who needs advice about the emotional matter is just as needy as a beggar on the street. Help people without expectations and feel the contentment your actions bring. You are helping them not you, but you will find personal worries will seem insignificant as a result.

Chapter 2: Identify your Worries and Deal with Them

Are you plagued by worries? Do you lay awake at night thinking about problems and overthinking certain aspects of your life? You are not alone, everyone has concerns and worries but it is how you deal with them that is important. There are certain things that life is just too short to worry about.

How to deal with problems that we all face

1) Finances: as the saying goes the only guarantees in life are death and taxes. That doesn't mean you should let either worry you so much that you lose sleep. Bills and money are both things that need to be addressed but here are a few tips to help you deal with them in a calm and sensible way:

   - Create a personal budget based on your income and your outgoings. Seeing your details in black and white will help you cut back on any unnecessary spending and review your finances.

   - Cut any bills that are "luxury" If your income isn't stretching enough to pay for unessential bills then you need to cut them. Cable tv is not essential, neither is Amazon Prime, Netflix or other prime entertainment options. There is a plethora of entertainment options to choose from that are free.

   - Prioritize your debts: Payback any outstanding loans to family and friends and avoid resentment. Debts to utility companies and banks can be negotiated but your friends and family will always be there for you when you need them.

- Pay your mortgage/rent: Keeping a roof over your head is the main concern. Your car and other concerns can wait.

2) The Past: History is an interesting subject but sometimes we can be haunted by our own personal history. The past is important, but it cannot be changed. What has happened is in the past and should not be a burden that affects your future. The only way you can be affected by your history is if you let it happen.

3) Negative influences: Social media and the world of "celebrity culture" has given rise to a new brand of human beings. "Haters" are all around us, people who believe they are entitled to say whatever they like about whoever they choose. Haters are not just concerned with famous people and chances are you will encounter negativity from people daily. If you let their attitude and comments affect you and cause you to stress you will never achieve anything. Don't stress the haters! Gossips are also a scourge on society and should be treated as such. It is great to talk with friends and family about their lives and what is going on with them but when they share details of other people's personal details it is time to walk away. Nobody trusts a gossip; they often have a negative destructive effect and rarely have a good word for anyone.

4) Aging: Getting old is scary. In your mind, you still feel like a youngster, but the mirror tells a different story! However, there is nothing you can do about it and you are going to age no matter what. Stop worrying about your impending journey into old age and instead embrace it. Accept the laughter lines and grey hairs and stop wishing you were younger, do fun things that you couldn't do in your youth and make the most of your time on earth. If you are still young and wish you were older then you must stop wishing your life away and make the most of your youth!

5) Death: The Grim Reaper is a figure that represents the inevitability of your impending death and cannot be dodged. Stop worrying about your mortality and what happens after you die and start living life to the full.

6) F.O.M.O.: The fear of missing out is a constant worry for some people and can ruin their social life. Social media allows us an unprecedented view of other people's activities and can lead to us convincing ourselves we are missing out on something. Stop worrying about what others are doing and walk your own path. Nobody else is going to pay your bills and put food on your table so focus on yourself.

7) What if's: Have you ever said something like this "What if I go to the store today and there is a robbery, and someone gets shot"? "What if I break down in the car and get stranded". If fear keeps you from doing anything you need to start acting and stop procrastinating. Fear is difficult to conquer but you need to realize that no matter how well you plan stuff

there is a chance it may go wrong. This should not stop you from doing it!

8) Mistakes: If someone tells you they never make mistakes then they are lying to you. Fact. Nobody's perfect and the trick is to learn from your mistakes, figure out what caused it and improve the way you do things in the future. Making a string of mistakes can be frustrating and disheartening but if you let these feelings affect you the idea of failure will overwhelm you. Clear your mind and reconsider the task in hand, ask advice if needed and start with a fresh slate.

9) Anything beyond your control: Do you find yourself getting annoyed by things that are out of your control? Do you get aggravated by the weather, traffic and natural disasters? Just ask yourself why! You can have a measure of control over these things but merely your own perception and attitude. Reduce your stress levels and focus on things that are pertinent to your life. The weather will be the same even if you aren't worried about it so carry on with the task in hand and just let nature get on with it.

10) Perfection: We all want to be the best version of ourselves, but we all have flaws. Accept that your faults are part of your make up and stop wasting your time trying to be perfect. If you fill your life with stuff that makes you feel fulfilled and happy you will soon realize that having a perfect life is not your goal. A happy life is much more fulfilling and even mistakes can be fun!

If your life is stuck in neutral, try sitting down and clearing your mind for 10 minutes. Close your eyes and picture yourself in a restful place, the beach, your favorite chair or even floating in a warm bath. Whatever relaxes you? Drop all the "problems" in your life from your mind and remember, life is too short to worry about...

Chapter 3: What are Positive Affirmations and How Can we use Them?

Consider your childhood. Were you surrounded by love and affection? Did you have a happy childhood and form lasting bonds with friends at school? If you had an idyllic childhood, then why do you have negative feelings about yourself and fail to realize your own potential?

The answer lies in our cultural heritage. The feelings of fear and guilt if you didn't conform come from guardians and authority and unless you had amazing people telling you how special you were then these feelings will follow you into adulthood.

It is rare for a child to be encouraged to be unique and special. Instead, we are taught to follow the rules and be obedient, you may dare to dream but society teaches you that these dreams will remain unfulfilled.

So, how can you become a fiercely positive being who lives life to the full and casts aside negative thoughts? Using affirmations may seem a little off the wall but telling yourself to be positive can be an uplifting process and ultimately increase your happiness and confidence in less than a week.

Affirmations should be used in the present tense and if possible, should be said loudly and consciously. Embrace the words that you use and believe in them!

Here are some situations that may arise and some suitable affirmations to use

When you are feeling insignificant or overwhelmed by life

1) I am a unique citizen of the world
2) I matter and my presence is a gift
3) I have a brightness that shines and casts light on the world

When you are nervous

1) I am strong enough to get through this
2) I am able to breathe in calmness and exhale nervousness
3) I believe in myself and my ability to shine

When you are angry

1) I can visualize my anger and let it go
2) I am able to replace my anger with positive emotions
3) I accept responsibility for my anger, but I can forgive myself

When you feel hopeless and at the end of your tether

1) I accept the situation and will try to find a positive aspect
2) I possess the optimism to find hope in any situation
3) I will explore all ways of coping
4) If I have exhausted my options I will ask for help, this is not a weakness
5) I have inner courage that helps me cope

When you are with people you love

1) I am surrounded by people who love me and respect me
2) I feel safe and respected among my friends
3) I take the time to show my friends what they mean to me
4) I enjoy the differences in opinions we all have and respect their beliefs
5) I don't judge others and my friends do not judge me

When you are among strangers

1) I am smart and good company; these people are in for a treat
2) I am sure I am going to meet someone amazing today
3) If I feel the need to leave, I have the confidence to do so
4) I see myself as a gift to the world
5) I refuse to compare myself to anyone for I don't know their whole story

When you can't face the day ahead

1) I choose to give this day my full consideration and face it with joy
2) My mind is capable of creating a bright new day
3) This day holds no fears and will bring me nothing but happiness

When people are unsupportive to your dreams

1) I will answer questions about my dreams without becoming defensive
2) I accept the choices of others but will not let them affect me pursuing my dreams
3) I follow dreams no matter what the obstacles

When you are at work

1) I choose to work here, and I find the work fulfilling and enjoyable
2) I am responsible for my career success and see myself advancing through my own hard work
3) My job impacts other people in a good way
4) I can influence others with my experience
5) I am a key part of a successful operation

When you can't sleep

1) I thank my mind for all its great work during the day
2) I now release my mind from thinking and wish it a good night
3) I am surrounded by the peace and quiet of the night
4) I look forward to the pleasant dreams that await me
5) A full night's peaceful sleep lays ahead

When you are sad and lonely

1) I am surrounded by the love of those who are not physically present
2) Solitude is a gift and allows me to enjoy my own company
3) I am too big a gift to the world to feel sadness or self-pity

When you are tempted to give up

1) Giving up is an easy option and I am better than the easy option
2) I will carry on because I believe in the task, I am attempting

3) My goals have no time limit and it is too early to contemplate giving up
4) I know what lies ahead is worth the effort so I will press on
5) I am willing to try every conceivable option

When you doubt yourself

1) I am not just good enough; I am better than that
2) I approve of myself and that is all that matters
3) I no longer have the habit of self-criticism
4) I am able to see the benefits of my flaws and my personal gifts
5) I have a positive mindset and am able to praise myself

When you feel stuck in a rut

1) I know the answer is available to me, I just need to keep looking
2) I am actively looking for ways to change my situation
3) My abilities will help me unlock the way and set me on a new path
4) I have the courage to try a path that is completely new
5) My mind will always embrace new ideas and concepts

When you recognize your own awesomeness

1) I leave behind my past; it has no power over me now
2) Everything I need will become available to me at the right time and place in my existence
3) My heart and my mind have a rhythm that flows, and I embrace it fully
4) I am gifted and talented, I matter to myself and others
5) I am deeply fulfilled with my life and who I am

These phrases will help you leave behind the negative feelings that can hold you back. You can also use them to inspire you in the home or workplace. Most furniture or décor stores will have bright colorful signs that you can hang on your walls, here are a few personal favorites that hang in my home:

- Follow your heart
- Create peace
- Dream big
- Enjoy the little things
- Hug often
- Do your best
- Say I love you
- Laugh at yourself
- Be spontaneous
- Fall in love
- Show gratitude

Chapter 4: Surround Yourself with Positivity

Are your surroundings energizing? Are the people you have around you filled with positive energy and give you joy? Sometimes it doesn't matter how you are feeling these outside influences can just drag you down and leave you feeling insecure and empty.

Consider the people in your life, do some people just leave you exhausted after spending time with them? You know the type, energy suckers! Imagine a vampire that feeds on energy and leaves you flat and lifeless once they have fed. The thing is, these people are a direct reflection of your own personal beliefs about yourself.

They are drawn to you because they sense your insecurities and use them to feed their own negativity. So, what can you do to change the type of people that are drawn to you? The good news is that as you improve your self-belief you also improve your vibes. This will attract more positive people to you and improve the energy that surrounds you.

Simply put if you have negative feelings of self-doubt you will attract the energy vampires yet if you feel great about yourself you will attract positive energy.

Here are three life-changing tips to attract positive people to your "vibes"

Believe in yourself

Think of the people you know who are self-confident and positive. You are immediately aware that they have confidence that shines like a light in a dark room. Accept who you are and embrace your strengths, talents, and abilities. Have a daily talk with yourself and be kind. Tell yourself you look great and that outfit looks amazing on you. Be positive and you will attract positive relationships.

Forgive freely

Holding a grudge is a surefire way to display negative energy. Forgiving people is not a weakness, in fact, it is a strength. Letting go of resentment and emotional pain frees you from becoming stuck in the moment. Once you have forgiven yourself or others for mistakes you are free to explore a future free from negative memories. Recognize that you can learn from difficult life lessons and grow as a person and you will shift to higher energy plane. This, in turn, will attract like-minded people into your life.

Appreciate others

Sharing appreciation of others encourages them to grow closer to you and form stronger bonds. Celebrate the success of others and encourage them to reach greater heights instead of feeling resentful of their success. When you achieve your goals, you will have supportive set of friends just waiting to help you celebrate as well!

It is highly rewarding to be surrounded by positive people, but it takes practice. When you feel a negative thought entering your space you must replace it with a self-affirming thought. Make it a natural practice to think of yourself as a magnificent being and at home with other magnificent people!

Of course, your relationships are significant but there are other ways to create positivity around you. Here are some simple tricks to introduce a positive element to your surroundings.

Nature

A display of fresh flowers can lift even the dullest room. Bringing nature into the home or workplace can be refreshing and give you a positive focus. A potted plant or a bouquet of spring flowers will look great on your desk or in your living space. If you have allergies or other restrictions, you can use natural fabrics or materials to create a calming environment. A beautiful wooden bowl or a cashmere throw will allow you to appreciate nature's beauty.

Visual aids

Having a visual perception of your positivity surrounding you is essential. Display framed photos of your family and loved ones will help you tackle difficult times and motivate you. Maybe you are inspired by people in the media or even places you want to visit. Use your goals to motivate you by placing images in your eye line. They will help you put in the extra effort if you are feeling down and just need some motivation. Surround yourself with beauty and fond memories and you will always have a smile on your face!

Music and media

What you see around you is important but so is what you hear. If music is your passion, then make powerful playlists to suit different occasions. Choose inspiring, high energy tracks to listen to when you need a boost. Have a playlist to relax to, even one to eat too! If you love music use it to inspire you and carry you to the next place. The beauty is you can take it just about anywhere, the car, the gym, work, and home. If music isn't your thing you can listen to other types of audio, try an inspirational speech by someone you admire. Catch up on current affairs by tuning into news outlets and informational podcasts. The bottom line is don't neglect your ears!

Quality entertainment

How you spend your leisure time should also be considered. Pick up a good book and immerse yourself fully for a couple of hours. Self-help books are great but sometimes you just need to lose yourself in a great story. Become the hero and learn how to adapt their qualities to help your own personal journey. Alternatively watch some quality TV or a movie. There is a wealth of excellent shows and movies that can help you enjoy your downtime and also be inspired.

Spread positivity

Be free with compliments and give genuine feedback to others. If someone does something that you find impressive then share your sentiments. Even holding the door open for someone can make their day. Giving up your seat and offering to allow someone to go in front of you in a queue may seem insignificant but they are both positive twists on life. Volunteering is a great way to give back to the community and spread positivity. Helping people less fortunate than yourself will also help you appreciate what you have and the love that surrounds you.

Quotes

Positive affirmations help you reach higher levels of positivity and should be used daily (we will cover this later!) but quotes can also inspire you. Create your own personal life motto and display it prominently, use inspirational words from your favorite people. Avoid negative energy by surrounding yourself with positivity. These quotes can also be amusing, life doesn't have to be too serious, take a look at these funny life quotes:

"You know you're old when the candles cost more than the cake" Bob Hope

"The fact we're all different is the one thing we have in common" Justin Young

"Stop worrying about the world ending today, it's already tomorrow in Australia" Charles M Schultz

If you are looking for inspiration the world is an open book! Search for words to inspire you and fill you with hope and use them daily.

Chapter 5: Rewire your Brain for Positivity

It is natural and normal to think negative thoughts because your brain automatically generates them. However, you do have the power to change the way your mind works and reset your default way of thinking to positive.

Automatic negative thoughts can be overwhelming and make you feel anxious and depressed. They are not pleasant, but you can deal with them and change the narrative.

How you deal with negative thoughts

You need to realize that they are

- Not true
- Unhelpful
- Designed to keep you from moving on
- The key reason you feel anxious or depressed

Automatic negative thoughts

"Always trust your feelings" is fine for some people but when your first response is a negative one does this mean you should believe it? No, it doesn't. Recognizing this fact can change your life and your thinking. Consider the following phrases and if you automatically think like this then you need to rewire your thoughts:

Someone gives you a compliment about your appearance and you think: "They don't mean it" or "They must be lying"

Something great happens to you and you hear this phrase in your head; "Why me, I don't deserve this" or "Something will happen to take this away from me"

You meet a group of strangers and you think: "They will all hate me and wonder why I am here" or "Nobody wants to meet me, I'm not good company"

You need to challenge these thoughts and recognize that automatic responses are not truthful. You must stop them from running your life and making you miserable. The next time you have a negative thought ask yourself one simple question, "How true is this thought?" and then analyze the answer.

For instance, take the phrase "nobody likes me" that can often crop up in our thoughts. Replace this with a deliberate thought such as "ok, have I met everybody in the world, the country or even my town? No, I haven't, neither has there been a survey done on my likeability so how can I think nobody likes me?" Doing so allows you to distinguish between what you believe and what you know. This is a positive way to think and helps you dispel the automatic negativity in your mind.

There are multiple ways to deal with them and these two examples could be the ones for you:

1) Imagine the thoughts are outside your head: This technique allows you to manage the thoughts and decide what to do with them. Once any negativity begins to form just refuse to let it in. State clearly and

with conviction "No, I refuse to allow negative thoughts to enter my head". Repeat the word "no" until the thoughts disappear.

2) If you find it difficult to dispel the thoughts try adding words to them to change the narrative. For instance, if your thought is "I hate my job and I am terrible at it" add positive elements to form "I hate my job so I am going to look for another, I know that I am good at....." Another way to change perspective can be "Life is pointless" will become "Life is pointless if you don't make the most of it".

Negative thoughts often occur at regular times of the day or are triggered by certain locations. Knowing what triggers your negative thought process can help you be more alert and ready to deal with them.

Programming your brain to be positive

Now we understand what negative thinking is and how to deal with it we have taken the first step to rewire the brain. The following exercises will expand on the process and allow the brain to be happy and recognize success. We can also overcome bad habits and make it easier to improve life in general.

Follow these tips to rewire your mind for positivity

1) Recognize that you view positive and negative thoughts simultaneously: George Orwell created a term in his groundbreaking novel, 1984, called doublethink and described it as the process of holding two opposing thoughts in one's mind and giving them

both the same consideration and acceptance simultaneously.

Doublethink describes perfectly the way your brain works when considering positive and negative thoughts. It values both and uses them to fit the situation. For instance, your brain can create thoughts that indicate a positive attitude to yourself. "I am a valuable member of society" and "I have no qualities to offer the world" are two opposite opinions but can be given the same value in your head.

Rewiring your brain means you place less value on negative thoughts and automatically favor positive thoughts instead.

2) Identify your goals: Despite the phrase "seeing is believing" when setting goals in life we first must believe in them before we see results. Examine your goals and how they will manifest in your life. Believe that you will achieve them and imagine how your life will be when you have all you wish for.

3) Embrace positive emotions: Emotions are the fuel of the mind; they power our minds and bodies to strive for greater things and better intentions. Positive affirmations are only helpful if they stir the emotions and fire up the spirit. What emotions do you associate with accomplishments? Pride, happiness, elation or joy are all emotions we love to embrace. Recognize what your goals mean to you and imagine the surge of emotion you will feel when you achieve them.

4) Visualize: Your brain is the starting point for forming new habits. If you visualize images that accompany your goal, then your mind automatically increases your ability to create them in life. If you are

committed to a future that is positive and fulfilling the images you create in your mind should reflect this. You will then begin to shape your actions to create a positive outcome you desire.

5) Make your actions reflect your intentions: It is one thing to imagine positive actions but unless you actually make changes to your routine it will just be hot air! For instance, if your affirmations are all about eating healthier and getting yourself fit there is no point sitting down and eating burgers every day. There is also no point going to the gym but complaining about it. Rewiring your brain means embracing your new goals and experiencing positive emotions as you do so.

Of course, this process requires commitment and practice. You have a lifetime of overthinking and negativity to overcome. Think of it in the same way you train a puppy: you need to catch it pooping on the carpet to house train it. This is how you rewire your brain; you catch it in the act of forming a negative thought and change the process.

Chapter 6: What are the Benefits of a Positive Lifestyle?

Having a positive attitude is an attribute that enhances your daily life but how does it impact your overall health? Does it improve any other areas of your life and if so which areas? Here are some interesting facts about how positive thinking can change certain areas of your life:

Health and wellbeing

We know that having a positive mental attitude makes life more enjoyable, but have you considered the fact that it can actually add years to your lifespan? There are great benefits to cutting out negativity and overthinking but what are the physical health benefits you can expect to feel?

1) Boost your immunity: Studies have shown that your mental thinking can affect your immune system. Participants who display positivity and optimistic thinking had a strengthened immune system. Participants who displayed pessimistic tendencies had a less responsive immune system and were more prone to illness.

2) Increased resilience: If you believe you can cope with whatever life throws at you then you will be better equipped to recover from actual traumas and crises. If you can remain positive when faced with tough times you will be able to recover from the ordeal quicker.

Negativity will lead to longer recovery and greater stress.

3) Reduce stress: Positive thinking is the perfect way to manage stress levels and reduce the impact they have on health. The way you think impacts directly on stress levels and help our bodies avoid stress-induced conditions.

4) Reduce blood pressure: One of the greatest problems faced by people is high blood pressure that accompanies increased levels of stress. Removing anxiety and negativity will help you lower your blood pressure and lessen the chance of heart disease.

So, what does changing your mindset achieve for your health? Basically, optimists live longer! Positive thinking can add years to your life!

Success in the workplace

If you can change the way you think you can also achieve success in your career. Imagine if all your perceived problems became opportunities and enabled you to progress. When you realize that all problems are solvable to some degree you completely change how you perceive obstacles. You will soon become a "go-to" person and will rise through the ranks of your chosen career.

Motivation boost

Positive thinking can give you wings! You will begin to realize that your personal goals are achievable and rather than wondering if you can achieve goals you will wonder when you will achieve them. You will also become appreciative of your surroundings and the company you keep. This realization will motivate you to block any negativity entering your personal space and interfering with your mindset.

Harmonious relationships

How many people remain stuck in toxic relationships just because the alternative seems much worse. Once you realize that being alone or single is not a punishment or unpleasant you will be able to let go of relationships that cause you pain and sadness. Your improved mindset will attract a new type of person. This is known as the law of attraction when "like attracts like" and can bring joy and happiness to your personal relationships. Your close friends and even your partner will benefit from a positive mental connection and your relationships will thrive. Knowing that you can share your dreams and innermost thoughts with those that you love, no matter what their reaction, is priceless. Losing the fear, we have of other people's opinions will free your mind to explore new options.

Create a better first impression

How do you think people perceive you when meeting for the first time? Do they see someone who is interesting and fun to know? Although you are not affected by negative thoughts your new positive attitude will give you the confidence to make a great first impression. People, in general, are drawn to friendly, kind and non-aggressive personalities and feel at ease from the first contact.

First impressions can help you develop in many ways. Expand your social circle, meet new dating options or simply get on better with your co-workers. Your family life should also benefit from your new attitude and any past disagreements can be cast aside and forgiven.

Improves focus and concentration

When you think positively you free up the part of your mind that would be held back by pessimism. When doubt creeps in and tells you that what you are trying to do is impossible then part of your mind is occupied with these thoughts. Dispelling the negativity means you focus all your energy on getting the job done.

Negative thoughts are energy thieves and steal away your peace of mind. Making the choice to think valid, positive ways to benefit yourself will concentrate your focus on achieving your goals. Your mind will clearly show you how to go forward and refuse to be hampered by indecision or doubt.

Happiness

The feeling of better health improved personal relationships and success in both personal and work-related goals can only lead to one thing. A happier you. The more value you place on your life then the happier you become and the more you enjoy life to the full.

Inner beauty

Who do you admire for their beauty and attraction? Ok, mean and moody film stars aside, the most attractive people in life are smiley happy people who seem to have an inner light that makes them glow. You will benefit from this inner glow once you rid yourself of negative influences. Your eyes will shine with hope for the future, your skin will glow from your healthier life and your smile will light up the room. Your posture will improve as your self-confidence grows and you will carry yourself with the bearing of a winner.

These benefits are only a drop in the ocean of the possibilities available to you. You have just dipped a toe, get ready to dive right in and bathe in the benefits that a positive mental attitude will give you. Optimism and positivity are the two most important skills you can possess and the only person holding you back is yourself!

Conclusion

Life is too short to waste on negativity. As you become a positive person you will also affect the people who surround you. If you always wanted to be that person who lights up a room and other people seem genuinely pleased to see, then now you have the tools. Change the way you live is a sweeping statement, but the power of positivity and great decisions does exactly that. There is a different way to live and you are now ready to take that journey. Good luck with your new future, you will do great things!

Thank you for reading this book

I hope you enjoyed it and got something useful from it. . Could you leave a review on Amazon.com? It'd be greatly appreciated!

Thank you and regards!

www.ingramcontent.com/pod-product-compliance
Lightning Source LLC
Chambersburg PA
CBHW050710250726
48662CB00002B/949